Fashion Coloring

Copyright © 2017 Brown

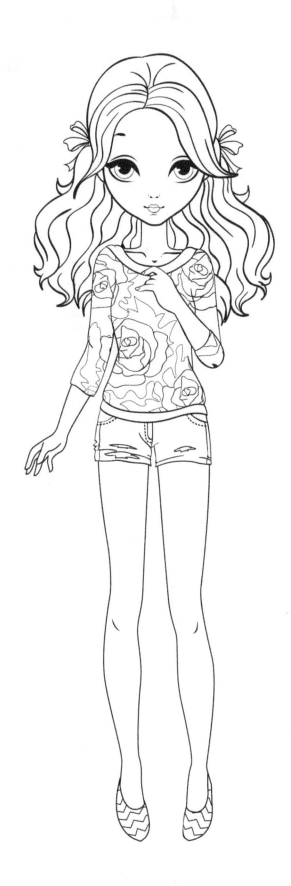

Thank you so much again for buying this book! I hope you enjoyed coloring my book. Now I'd like ask for a *small* favor. Could you please take a minute or two and leave a review for this book Amazon. It'd be greatly appreciated! And I truly value your opinion and thoughts and I will incorporate them into my next book, which is already underway.

CPSIA information can be obtained
at www.ICGtesting.com
Printed in the USA
LVHW022030260820
664093LV00001BA/4